the diary of an

elolita

plumalia henson

Plumalia Henson
plumaliapress@gmail.com

ISBN 979-8-218-69493-7 (trade paperback)

First Printing, June 2025

Cover artwork created by Tara Grace, 2025
Cover designed by Indole Noise Designs and Caleb Tucker, 2025

Printed in the United States of America.

Other Works by Plumalia Henson

POETRY
The Book of Venus

who is elolita, anyway?

elolita

elolita

elolita

elolita

elolita

do your bones ache when you beg, mister? is your age
catching up to you in all of your childish na-ture as you kneel
to my height/ knowing i will grow and you are finished/ does
it make you afraid of me? in the tall grasses of my snake-
infested psyche i see you standing beside me, i see you/
holding my hand, and how large/ your wet eyes do marvel at
how like a baby bird i can be/ how absolutely disgusting my
regurgitated thoughts appear/ but how simple to pick out the
sharp and silver bits and string me/ together a bracelet that
spells y-o-u-r-n-a-m-e/ that crusts and rusts itself and shimmers
as a sunset chasing the blood of my wrists/ as i have/ as i
have/ as i have/ the blood of my thighs/ how vampiric in
nature/ how like a creature of the night in communication,
how ghostly you are/ in red-tongued transgression/ a hunter

i understand religion now/ the hands of god lead me to destruction/ and they grip me so tightly i must confess i sweat a little to know i have no control/ my faith is starving as the nights near always/ i wonder if this will be my end but of course/ of course/ of course, it never is/ the sibling day arrives with my crumpled prayer clasped tight damp bleeding ink tattooed between my palms/ just like sleepwalking sleepwalking sleepwalking towards a danger that finds me/ unaware/ otherworldliness is enticing for the fear that coats it/ sticky and slimy fear/ it is only fear that turns my stomach so/ the blade is coming the blade is ever drawing closer and my lord is ever growing stronger and my light is fading fading so quickly my eyes fail to bleed within new-found sheet-black enveloping/ woolen is the blanket that wets with despair/ how strange for a man to claim devotion to a lifetime of depth of emotion and character/ and then fail to find me buried beneath the bottom of it all

elolita

she shows me everything
perfect-ly
so well-practiced
such a quieted form
she tells me everything
bears punishing as a daughter
blood beads poppy sweats through mine palms
and i think of her - to sleep alongside her
my chest stalls its rumbles in idling hours before
my day turns browned
and i think of her - to care for her
i crash and burn before false oblivion marred by
truth and edging towards a
delicately-placed
ending and i am resolute
in my consuming of her -
to protect her within myself
and she endures it all
perfect-ly

stare at duskish sky and beg for forgiving/ stare at the dirt beneath the feet and beg to be save-swallowed/ i wonder, if both were to be promised simultaneously, if the pure of making love between suffering and salvation would steam in finale inhale-exhale, exhale/ if the wet and wooded night-shade would hold the pieces firm so i may endure a clean severing of the spine and/ breathe/ but the earth is so plainly still/ it is only i that shakes and quivers as the morning grass would do/ once did/ the lights are glass walls pressing firm against my trachea/ and it chokes my heart full up and tightening/ my heart feels choked-/ about to-/ about to spew rare-red blood all about the hands of those/ those men who foolishly reached to aid in endeavors they would have to peel off their skin and implant fat beneath every layer of pore until gelatinous bursting bubbling disgusting leaking/ would have to climb a barefoot mountain to tumble naked down, again, again, again/ they cannot understand the warring enemy in the nerves that guide me/ the vein-ed leash/ they cannot feel it the way her body feels it/ and they cannot become small enough to beg

elolita

i cannot be a fleshy shield to hide sex addiction from
wandering morality/ that second-handed wickedness replicates
an anxious grief/ settles itself in bubbles of marrow/ it is too
strong it pierces and hurts/ but you love me/ you love me/
you love me/ yet carved into the sticky-wet waving of your
mind i cannot find my self as i know it to be/ cornered/
darkened/ is a thin girl dangling from a hook leaking liquid
life/ a filet striped infection fount built fresh, run dried/ run
dry/ your self-proclaimed animalistic nature and/ desire to
confront convention that colors me save-d/ savior complex
stripping me of the cage that kept/ keeps/ kept me from your
peeling fingers

Plumalia Henson

it feels like bondage it feels it
feels/ it feels like you have
torn my lord's gentle
forgiveness from my
outstretched hands/ aching/
so neither of us may have it/
it feels like i should not be
knowing it at all

elolita

the drags in my skin go un-answered
leaves my heavied heart second-guessing
while my heavied head wearies of waiting
waiting to be exalted divinely by her

and it has always been the excuse that frightens
leaves a tired man wondering of her mouth and
pouting heart-shaped for another but
those glossed lips bitten reddish-raw do cry
for no body in pain but i

she spares no detail of living
and i offer mine in entirety the same
wrapped inside innocence of a
finger-knotted promise that
nobody may know

elolita

twirling and twirling in weak-ness and will-powerlessness/ i
am salad-tossed within skull/ melting into my three-quarters-
sugar, one-quarters-coffee/ i adore these little motions of
picturing hurt and re-enacting grief/ i enjoy caressing my dry
cheekbones as though a man is wiping my tears/ for i will
never date in this era of purity and cleanliness/ i will only be
lifted from my heels and placed gently onto the lap of
someone who can care and have and love and hold/ a multi-
tasking agent of the entertwine/ a braider man

video girl has longer legs/ video girl has precious pink
pigtails/ video girl looks nothing like me/ shares nothing with
me but your affection and incredulous desire in distorting
pupil/ i have never known reckoning as this/ never tragedy/
yearning longs for my sweetness in the face cherubic/ white-
cotton flung to fence thrown to the wind on chicken-line
swaying/ i am made of fancies and fate-twine/ i can be
cinematic when i turn hip and bare side/ and i am horrific
when numbing my knees to hurry it all up now and please
please please/ please? picture me

elolita

dreaming always of you, my darling
mine spiced-scenting evergreen
mine
mine
and caught just before your age-d prime-
my, how brilliant was i?
how dainty with the netting a bud
of fragility a flower of naivete of purity
virtuous lamb-hood weakness affirmed
makes me marked a human god in selfless
selfishness
creating only you in the prettiest image
molding
you for my willing self sanctified
little mind-nurseling of mines

goodness dripping from the sky in small silvery pelleted rain
bullets fiercely biting at chilled skins - it rains so fierce i feared
the white-hot hand would snatch me/ maybe i wished but to
what/ to remain standing/ in my knee socks and training bra/
in the center of a field wispier than the baby's breathing
lachrymose, impatient/ with sink-mouth cavernously opened
and expectant as a piglet/ but all to be left for the swallowing
when turn comes is agony and the burrs that tear into my
tights/ trudge back home in spikes/ home to him/
underserving and understanding i am far from gone/ but
stretched in the opposite/ he cut my hand in a squared shape
and committed atrocities with my mangled flesh and now
swirling cut-print lingers scab flaked on my own body but i
still do not think i did that i do not think/ that could have
been my faults fissuring in that shape/ cracking the earth wide
open so i may fall into you

elolita

the dandelion does not know of death 'fore it watches the
living as it leaks all milky-whitened from its own slaughter-
slash-ed neck, thus i bear witness to my very own dirtying of
the severed limb/ i could not have known it would be this
way when i was littler - i do not think i dreamt/ this cherry
orchard haven of violence where i am felled and buckling to
the squish-squish-pop beneath him/ he who licks at me with
such a strange digging such molestation like he breathes only
tartness and exudes bitter/ i become bitter'd too

my virtue/ i lament it-/ my innocence dissolved-/ oneness in
the amniotic/ fluid and drunk through/ swallowed by the
mother of all this madness which bore i/ bore me already
disgusting/ nothing even to show but love like a porno-
graphic film violent and warring/ relentless and uncomfortable
deep i stand naked at cliff's edge/ a rake with heels so torn
and bleeding raw skin rawed further/ red-ring-ed irises
viciously glare a prayer, a prayer/ chewing at my self tearing
nail from bone from blood is the closest i have yet come the
approximate leaking intersection of our body transformed
within my desire to devour/ yours to watch/ our shared
wanting to destroy me but the world could swallow me in
such a way where anguish feels like emptiness and emptiness
feels like loveliness and loveliness lies loathe floating lyme in
death-stilled waters/ purity could become of me if i could just
cease-/ the unfurling of my tongue as a leaf/ the butterfly-ed
flicker of eye as down, i descend into whore-hood/ down, i
descend into the desire-able again

elolita

he shall not scream but he will purchase eight foot measures
rope/ rehearse his penmanship/ request i belong to him at
odd hours/ he shall not scream but he silently promises to
stain me forever-more-/ by forcing me bear witness to his
mind all wrong and dirtied/ his unwashings and undoings
done

always with the asking, it is/ in the saccharine lilting tones/
what i want/ as if he knows not/ as if you did not tell that
very truth to me while cupping face between rough hands/
what i yearned for/ as if you did not force a bone-stretch of a
metamorphosis inside me an awakening that of which no fear
had been previously incited/ but now i am terrified/ i am
scared of you with your hands/ and your eyes like hands/ and
your tongue like hands/ using every part of your body to
reach reach reach into the velveteen plush within which mine
lamby-heart bleats/ find fear and stroke it in that way that
makes my bloodied hands sweat cold - my tired form shiver
fierce

elolita

there is so much fearsome i write it all sweat it all, out! out!/ i
find peace in the losing and vomit vomit vomit loosening salts
and trepidations-calories all across the floor my bared essence
pools betwixt tiles/ i cannot find myself, and to look means to
think means to fear/ cannot find myself/ think on this time as
though it has passed/ with the musings of swirling echoed
burn - that maybe i should someday tell the world of how i
went crazy when i allowed you turn my body into a man-hold
arsenal/ den of depravity and remorse

of course she knows not how
to hold a candle without burning
the innocence sparkles brilliant through
unsteadied gaze, un-steadier hand
glittering quake ignites me something violent
but the heated rage of a disciplinarian coils
when she withers from the task
of simply loving me
as a girl loves the father -
and not a petulant babe
spitting up hot wax all over clean dressings

elolita

all these bitch dog-women
cry, moan for false salve
while there is mine fresh fruit
clean-sliced and sweetened
blood-juice flowing
spoilt only by too much knowing
of the worldly cruelties
the un-locked door loosened
to allow a rough hand guiding
towards dazzling ruination and
teenaged resentment
as all women young learn in their
frangible years and carry in
breasts until bodies fall

with every lancet-sweep of my paled bruise-toned skin that
leech that is thirteen spirals itself deeper, deeper and youth
seems such a curse as regret grows heavy, threatens to leaden
my step to ensnare my mind/ i wonder, how many things will
i ask to be forgiven for when i am old/ wonder if i could even
kneel then to ask/ or would you deign my knees too sturdy
and break them to dustings/ to find me bent proselytizing for
another, when/ my imminently inescapable departure creates
in you a solitaire man/ a lonelied man/ that which of course
you never could have achieved without that annoyance that
was the swishing of my ribbon-tied hairs tangling up in teeth

elolita

private little bloomingdoll
sweet princess of devotion
why have you forbidden me my heart's
truest desire
my darling double-child when i love you
could you genuinely be so cruel?
and oh, do you not know
i burn for you for your maturity in essence
the childlike nature of your abandonment disappointing
little-one, i would so cut your hair in punishing if i could
only be present to hold it firm
your beauty will fade with every step you place between
your wanton body-ache and my outstretched arms
nothing more than a stupid girl dressed up in ill-fit
play clothing praying to be as some whore
all grown

Plumalia Henson

i touch the sparkling sharpness but do not caress it with the
gentle nature of a care-giver/ i am in control i am in control i
am/ i fight urges that feel like heavier bodies than mine could
ever bear could ever aspire to but it all could wash over me so
smooth if i could just/ brea-/ i am in control i am in control i
am in control/ -the breathe in and the breath out even if it
does not ever feel enough, you must, you MUST/ who are you
if not a silvery spirit fighting blind-/ who? my lung pinches
between rib-fingers as breathings slip away and stumble inside
and outside to scrape my screamed-to-hell throat/ as glass they
tumble and slice not near enough to choke it out of me
proper i am in control/ for the blood is inside me and the
warring wants of my kindness and my hostility, the thickening
urge to claw my own chest cage opened free my wretch heart
from the infinite of all this pain and how it hurts, it hurts-

elolita

it hurts.
i want to go home
i want to go home
i want to go home
/but i have had five homes and not one has fixed me up
good/ still i cannot see what there is yearning for/ just five
houses/ just a hand-print of places of not belonging/ so what
if maybe/ i want for the stars but fear the blackening dark of
the universe/ will never be satisfied, my equal/ and still, i
cannot help but cry and want to go home/ want my mommy
and daddy all of it in one piece and one place though never
has been any other way - what psychosis is this? for me to
assume the pain of some sicker dolly-girl i never have met/ i
am in control/ even when i do not want for it/ my decisions
burden me so and the outcomes leave a vibrant stain along
the questioning line/ o' pitiful mouth pitied/ biting how it asks
and asks things i never wished with any precious tooth nor
candle to know a single answer to

can i/ sorries
may i/ sorries
talk to you? sir/ sorries
call me a little girl again/ call me what i am not that which you
fear me to be/ what i am let me be that thing that thing alone,
and maybe i could assume a lamb's form while my predatory
nature is at rest so i/ may i/ take control of it all through your
steadier hands controlling me/ please

elolita

starried blood-spots freck beneath tire-line all that contains/ all
that remains of the sweetness of a birthday cake/ fresh vanilla
refluxively burns burns burns my heart/ tasting dry grasses
regretful vinegar-swallowing/ my tainted lense is filled up
flirtation - with life and death and strangers and death again,
again death/ it festers deeper and low/ again, death, it grows/
with the strength of a stubborn weed-vine it tangles all
through hopeful budding for love and lust in heavier ages/

you must understand/ understand i do fight that goodest fight
to bleed it out of me, a black infection but it finds new rooting
in the holes where i have tore out hair to chew over the ends/
in sleeplessness and nervous fleeing-spree/ all can be thought
is to be death/ why should i will myself a drink/ if i only will
wilt and leak it out/ why to eat if it will only propel my
treacherous traitor mind-heart forward another day/ one i do
not have brand-newed sateen oiled skin for/ gloves with
which to handle/ as the human heart toils rolling down the
sandpaper and my hands find new ways to wrinkle and dry
and peel from the washing over washing over washing over
over over-/ but help, the repetition gives proper weight in my
breast, pulls me down with purpose/ it all only serves to
leaden my heel when i can only wish to endlessly jump
upwards

elolita

the emptied masking of a bruised pair o' tights against bright
white light leaves a run down my thighs that reflects in the
corner of his eye/ leaves lover-less indents in dimpled
kneecaps as apples bitten all lazy and gummy/ two pale pears
squished through a wired fence/ i find my shaping
unappealing and lie in the same position for hours waiting to
become something different/ waiting for the one who will
always routinely disagree/ who can breathe a dusting of glitter
over the hatred i possess and garden and prune for my
draping skin that does the same - i feel it/ i feel it, so/ i feel
like a movie star to be displayed on such a blinding screen/
but i wish all i had done was able to be held in my hands,
now/ so i could strike a match against the teeth-texture of my
fading animal enamel burn it all away/ smoke away my
mistakes as they roll themselves into cigar-ettes and inhale
some certain life lesson i must of course/ within escape of
shadowed doubt/ be missing

just for a moment-
just for a moment-
just for a moment-
just a second i think i may overcome myself/ to become
something new and embarrassing/ but he has me leashed so
damn tightly i salivate at the novelty of becoming a tail-chaser/
the samest self i ever had been/ spinning silk-threaded in a big
round circle until the cessation of noteworthiness/ until i see
the beauty unearthing in a little girl in the tinny twinkling of
tangled earphones/ she twirls them flirtatiously/ all
choreographed and empty/ views the world through unpicked
lashes flirtatiously/ sucks her stomach in to fill her flaring rib
flirtatiously/ eternally breathless for it/ feeling like she is some
sort of spotted rash all the world is cradling to cry over,
enduring her kindly, wearily/ and it drags that little palest-
yellow of mismatch ringed beneath heavied blue eyes/ feeling
infancy is a thing so angry/ to be quieted and cured-/ until i
see it all reborn

elolita

life seems but a love letter to the things i shove down my own throat an open enrollment of greed, that is all anybody truly cares to know/ the sour taste on an empty stomach becomes acquainted with the stake-end of my toothbrush that sings distortions of a lullaby/ she shares the depth of her wounds and i scream-/ a vacuous sob and a competitive spirit/ there is solidarity there/ that nobody can kill themselves first without leaving a trail of chasing bodies bled out behind them/ no teenaged girl left behind to turn vampire licking infection in the school's bathroom, them - crook the neck/ salted ink/ and the nurse-cap knows it/ she knows it/ she wraps it up/ you wish she would condemn it properly so you may not utter it yourself, how damning/ but he/ he who hears me/ hears everything without mine speaking a word of it/ he hears it all inside of me when it rumbles

he somehow knows me bettered than i/ as if i am naked and
splayed all about a table with my skin pulled every which
direction to be inspected and claimed/ bandaged and kissed
like some corpse/ a necrophiliac simulation to uncover all
who i am no longer/ it is nice for a man to know you as your
maker/ it is nice to feel understood/ it is nice for a man who is
a god to know you/ but only ever nice, only ever nice

elolita

i find this peculiar transfiguration awfully quick and slick now/
when i look in those flesh corners where you rested palm and
spirit heavy/ i can only see a tragedy of lacking/ a lush hand
turned desert, the brine of mine mind sticks into the fresh
cracks in my lip/ body swells and breaks and yet it cannot hit
me with dirt/ no solid ground is to find me stationed
anywhere i recognize/ in the midst of this, you die/ and die/
and i-/ it is all feigned but who am i to know who am i to
know who i am without you/ a frail human girl with frail
human properties both chemical and emotional, wrong/ my
older sister younger sister mother father daughter and babe, i
am all relations to selfhood incarnate/ now i build us up in a
foundation of questions and shield it with my discolored spine
from any breathing of indifference/ now i just need to
understand why you could how what would when what
would inform you what what could encourage you to do such
a damned and dastardly thing/ lies - are a poison fertilizing the
deepest roots of dearer fears in my loosely-installed mind/ and
yet you lie lie lie lie lie

you only faked your demise but i
cannot say i faked the relief that
now, there would be no choice but
to give you up/ welcome back, my
tiring love, to my tired heart

elolita

do you ever think long or hard about who you are - that man
inside your mind that keeps you breathless and gasping to
suckling on nothing as you beg endlessly for the withering
oxygen as it leak-bleeds from stuck lung/ but he says to me,
he says that life shouldn't be about myself or my body/ and
that i would be a cruel and clever devil in my fracturing
youthful nature to hide it all from his leering/ comforting/
demanding insulting so incessant and firm in the shameful
solace of his glued gaze - now i find love in teachers and
fathers and older brother-men and still i/ do not find him
without reaching/ cannot touch myself without flinching, even
to wash my hair

infatuation is a heavy and thick noxious gas that burns and
blisters me plain-seared to hell/ a heavy and thick low-
hanging cloud that asphyxiates/ telling a girl what she wants
to hear is as throwing a chunk of her own flesh into her cage
and forcing the jaw to smack and feed with hands willed and
unrelenting because you dribble to hear in feigned
satisfaction/ i did not even know what i wanted before his
confidently assured self-appointment/ to be beneath him and
his sweltering blanket of love, love, love/ with the horrific
intensities of bitter wind ripping he must feel me 'round the
mind with chills inside and shivers skating oh, wide silver
rings on his digits as they rehearse their blind reaching/ and i
do confess, mama i had no idea when i was wee smaller that
men were infantile-d in this way/ shaken am i to witness over
pathetic tremble where i hold the illusion-pelt of confidence
lest it wrinkle by my doing, could not have bear'd it/ i thought
slick surety was in all of them, mama/ yet another way in
which i become wisened by all this, become older/ in learning
that men are only good as it relates to their skilled entrapment
of the underdeveloped heart

elolita

the rose-maple syrup between my fingers separates my heart
into colder chambers/ these sickened cells that i have
forgotten childish things for way of knowing him/ horror of
imagination has wild tooth and tongue far stronger than a fair
babe/ so i must grow taller to better breathe around it/ the
emptiness of spoken praise with nothing to hold can still leave
me breathless but pounds of sugar poured into that starving
bag of stomach nauseate and corrode/ my mother surely never
fed me in such a way/ i cannot swallow it save for the force-
push and first-shove he offers in assistance asphyxiation
aspirating dead/ i have not been sleeping well

Plumalia Henson

i have not been sleeping well
he has not sent me off with instructions for laying in days/ nor
have i suffered in the delights of watching the moon rise
through his littler windowed image/ obviously, he has forgot
me as they all do, when i turn in age and season/ when i fail
to keep them incubated warm within my bony'd bosom rest i
sit at the stes of his heart in a beggar's attire, and i do not ever
sit alone - my skin a blessing and my mind a curse, and i do
not sit alone/ i sit at those steps and i bed myself there and
pray to a god that knows me only how i want it to be/ for my
caging bloodlust to return to me and the false-hoods to enact
their crucifixions of me make something of the kindling thing
that will not rise from her stair/ please/ please/ please

elolita

the sir dares not speak to me on my bleeding days-
"remorseless body" he says and will not look
"cruelty lines you and scrapes at your insides" he says/ decrees
it to my nations of organs wretched/ i leak innocence and
swallow pain in rotten apple-seeds/ for a young woman is a
frantic porcupine spitting rage and fighting air and his hands
are scarred from spindle and peach-pitted from teeth/ a week
of it just six days week makes a weak little-one run frenzied
and animal-wild i know it - the large man fears gore on his
hands for it may stain his soul to never come off to never
come off no matter the abrasion replacing/ for me to be
touching him as a woman means something unsettling to him/
he shivers with anticipatory grief trepidation/ grief/ repulsed at
the thought of a potential turn of my mind/ sweaty and chilled
is he in acknowledging the painful truths of this world and the
wrongful nature of his own/ but I/ STILL/ LOVE/ HIM/ and
confusion is pouring from me now at a rate not even artery
can aspire to/ i still love him, of course/ my childhood is
forever the memory of loving him, of course/ and who? who
could i ever be/ who would i even become to abandon it all,
of course/ though, when the light shines on me i swear i am
already forgetting

i fail again
to cleanse myself
but i do wake to her
telling me she loves
me forever-
for ever-more
oh, like a songbird squeezing
within my loving embrace
how she cries in desperate
pathetic agonies
a baby-angel-thing clutching
me in quivering hold
always ever the one to be
so in pain, how lovely in pity
the guilt of almost stealing
that ache to leave her empty
sobers my dolorous tones with
the loveliness of ownership
i have you,
i have you,
i have you

elolita

there is something wrong within me
there is a great thing turned wrong-side in my brain for why
does my feeble vein flicker and purr when he whispers my
name/ when he covets me? calls me a terrible secret oh, no!/
there is nothing i could want more/ not water or air or tiny
little cake-pastries with zero caloric value in abundance just his
hot breath on my scalp/ as he cradles my head so tenderizing
and firm/ as if he knows also that even the awful truths of the
self are still the self therein contained/ that every part of the
self/ all my adoration only exists in the conjuring-space of my
wet brain so he protects my soul and all the while, my body
starves burns dies aches dissolves and peels, dies and breaks
once more

so many times i have called him by that name/ that simply
reading the word pulls the worn worm trigger-string of my
malformation and suddenly, i am both shivering and hot/ in
the shake there is a form of desolate survival tiny and birthed
white-soft/ that, overrides the wishings for heart-shaped lips
and a figure of pale bone emerges/ drags them back, drags me
down too and thirds my thirsts

elolita

a mouth is all i can be
tongue-splits to prod to pry
a syrup'd sugar cube, is she
dissolving within the sweat of mine
ever-watching eye
only my lick to guide her
only i can relieve
but a father-mother is all she does see
though her well runs every-day dry
a child of fiercest anger is she
so now she finds familiarity in my
guided by lustful love-full fear
with only my tear to chill her and
with only my hands to mistreat

he couldn't have been angry - for his mouth was so tremble-
turned downwards/ and his eyes were not red but pink-ed
and glowing with tragedy in the small vein/ he could not have
been angered for he does love me so and it circles 'rounded
us as fruit flies we/ mustly be so fresh and red to smell so
honeyed/ sweet a flight in search of the definition of nubility
flushed/ me hot with a disabling confusion and a volt of
instability stripping my stomach rendered me arrested in
collaring vulnerability inside my own/ shame-broiled fascia/
slapped with such a silence for days/ deserted, abandoned/
my punishment for personality/ personal preoccupation with
grand moralities and legalities and kindness such a danger/ a
wild, wild, salivating wolf of a man/ to fixate on the sweetness
he appeared so very engrossed with the idea/ of absorbing to
dissolving to controlling to destroying

elolita

i fall to pieces/ cradle them in my hands/ and weigh them/
sighs rumble throughout/ for seventy-five pounds/ and
unprettied rounds and there are ribbons in my body that flick
outward as the tongues of snakes/ on the ground/ in my
underwear/ ribbons! all around my throat and neck and chest
ribbons! in my skin as it withers snakely slithers whispers/
what is left? what is left what is left what is left?/ ribbons! for a
sinner's heart converted auto-cannibalistic/ ribbons! in torn
solidarity i starve and discard over and over and over/ and it is
all printed in numbers, oh, sweetly numbers, for it is always a
number that cuts me/ my life just like a ribbon

the free-flowing fountains of lust run rosy-scented and ever-fragrant/ i dream and sweat for you/ paint my cheeks valentine and heart and my lips all red-wined/ sitting with legs propped in that way where the fat on my thighs hangs below and peels itself from bones peeking through to their crowning shine all perfectly posed/ like the girls in the pictures with bodies like packs of cigarettes and glitter and balloons liquored stupid and last-night's mascara drawn fresh smudged down down down/ so chic in transparency so aloof in translucent shimmer/ crackling acetate vanity how lush/ to have that freedom to set your own body ablaze in such stale hedonism/ beautiful, they all are and i love the way their inability to open-close and gnash teeth and swallow sparkles right through them all

elolita

you tell me to behave and your tongue cradles itself/ against
your uneven bottom teeth and bridge breaching foam/ spits
on the syllables in such regard where i suspect you may not
actually desire that at all/ you do not mean it the way my
mother does/ do not know my body the way my mother
does/ do not want what is/ what is best for me?/ where is the
man with the silver-tooth fetish for kindness and holding my
hand to feel it pound a pulse - my blood as it races so
frantically to heat wherever you are nearest/ in my body
dilapidated and curdling/ why do you call me baby if not
simply to acknowledge my status/ why/ why/ why/ do you
call me yours?

baby-doll
baby-doll
where could you have gone-
my precious little-one
my lover of all things
faded into some evil ether
leaving my dissatisfaction mirrored
i never was even able to swallow
my angelic entree
and the taste of empty space has soured
in the choke between the back of my
tongue and throat

elolita

never had i considered before such a strangely romantic
prospect/ that i could have options outside of myself/ never
had i come to such a resolute conclusion/ to bloodlessly kill
myself betwixt sing-song cries of daddy, help me and daddy
save me as is crocheted in the vein-webbing hind my eyes and
branded before my youth by thousands of faceless hands not
unlike an idol/ not unlike a god, an ocean lapping tongue
before tongue after tongue it hurts worse if you lick the same
wound for/ long enough/ better to bandage and dispose/
better to cut fresh

too young to truly speak on my nature, but i do it anyways i have/ never been a reader of the conditions for our engagement/ a paper-cut skimmer of smaller prints/ but i am studious at the jagged knife-blades of my fingertips as they victimize my skin and brutalize me/ the caverns and craters of a little girl's face simply too much, too deep and dark and horrifying/ too unlike that elusive she-character/ the starlet in my cellular rendering me inadequate with a singular scan through dead eyes/ there is such nihilism in the language of her casually perfectly methodically casually posed body/ body/ body/ what of mine? what product could come of my flesh that would bring me into the room of cornucopias and kegs/ what gunpowder could i swallow to birth the fireworks that make her skin so radiant?/ can i be/ her/ her/ her/ be her instead of me?

elolita

little-one
little-one
from my fingers to my heart
i feel you snaking through
rooting yourself to the bumpy intersection that glues
my hands to my body, my hands to my body
i think of you when the night feels glittering
i can imagine your milk skin in the seam
ridgeline of my fingerprint, all moon-burned and clamped
in that peeling fantasy revelations betray my great epiphany
hatred is love and loving pain burns all alive within
but you will still think of me always
but still you will think of me always
but always, you still will think of me

Plumalia Henson

i am learning/ a student of life/ a poet of daughters/ that to be
elder is to be roped in scars with skin that weighs like bags of
sand that to be young is to be a teary-eyed and freshly-opened
sore always always always spread and raw and cherry-
reddened with hurting/ and to learn that of course, he holds
me down/ for i would float away if not for all the heft of him/
i am learning that i wish for him to tie me by my throat with
comparisons to any such smaller animal/ something
snappable/ lace-lined inside/ cleaner, girly, cleaner, still/ for
you to see yourself reflected in my eyes and think, cleared and
emptied so like a doe-ling little fox-rabbit-kitten monstrosity of
spirit convulsing in mewls/ rabidity in the round-face-ed
scowling i present/

elolita

and the grandmothers of us all cannot recall a time they
yearned to be injected with helplessness/ they must not have
feared themselves at this age/ they must have feared you,
instead/ but i, in my apple-cored backwards heart of a mind
all silly and gummy/ do not/ you, in your open cavern of a
maw of a mouth shaped and sharpened by greed and licking-
lip devotionals 'til the lip gets made gone/ shame is much
taller a shadow than you/ shame in eating the dirt and
swallowing it/ shame in reaching to cradle an animal wild to
hit it when it does not melt against your sweating palm/
shame as the photos the photos the photos/ shame in flushing
from a thudding fall while dancing sweaty and alone for none
oh/ i gag on the throat-closing choice of it all

something is haunting me
whispering truths in shrilly whistle within the wintering winds
a pink-tipped pearl of a hat pin shoved blunt-end firstly
through both ears until the nose bleeds brain all out/ eyes
freeze with damp encouragement a second-hand gifted/ but i
lay nude on the snowy bank/ i burrow my face as the rabbit
before me/ she is so beautiful, so thinning/ how the air makes
no room for her body to be but crackling fire ribs at the inhale
proclamation of a smoky exhale to answer it soonafter/ she
could never know how it feels to be an ugly dog/ forsaken
child/ first-drafted ink stain spoilt of a little boy stretched
down out about into the thousand-pound bone of an angry
man's forearm/ a breeding ground for breeding fantasy that
fattens quick and sinister/

elolita

solitude in sleep cradles me as he could/ i slept naked/ i sleep
with the door locked and my proximity to him tucked neatly
warmly beneath my rib stomach/ arms/ tangled within
themselves struggling to hold me with the heat intact/ safety
both eludes me and leaves me stricken in a profound
disorientation i touch/ my body at night and find a boredom
disease embedded/ both familiar and unknown in
implantation/ smooth and unforgiving in implementation the
simultaneous emerges/ at last in freedom to suffer/ as though
it could be that i have finally found that sickeningly unnatural
twist of the double-tongued devil in flesh that exists between
perdition and a fabled brighter light/ but the light is so small
square-d to square, so ten-dollar that you could almost miss it
- my inconsequential life's wholeness in lacking meaning

grief has taken me by the hair and dove fiercely into the dirtiest water/ cannot i be cleansed in my entirety of the jawslick of oily resentment and regret/ how it does cling and wet my eyes eternally 'til my lids are burning and purple-veined looking all out into the world i chose/ i see absolutely nothing of worth nor substance i see nothing at all now that you cannot reach me/ i am prickled in anticipation for the anger to come/ the spines of the doormat scrape and poke at my knees still-/ i am prickling in anticipation for the anger to come i am prickling in anticipation for the anger to come for anything/ better than this loveless watching and waiting, wailing/ finding myself inside of corn husks grounded and pot-holes and burned-down cigarettes fizzling to death inside a half-drunk crystal flasked - why, it stinks! burns my nostrils right to hell/ but neither of us are interested in my growing up/ only in me perfecting a pearl oasis amongst the ashes of your adulthood all sacrificed

elolita

why must men fear the chill in the wind when summer fades
when the rosy in a blush is as an island of blood amidst the
white pale/ are you truly so frightened of peeling/ your sun-
stained skin backways before your coarse grain peeling/ like
how the tree-bark curls/ and finding me nestled gently among
your arthritic tendons and kindling joints - when i find you
peering through every cell i have ever generated every second
i am awakened and aware of living in this solitary half-form?/ i
never thought it could be possible to become too familiar with
the danger of your tooth's thinning ledge, but the boredom of
a teenaged creature of poetry is far stronger than the girl who
bears it, far more powerful than any emotion that could have
come before it/ i am bored/ the boys are tiring of me and my
unwillingness to dance with them, and it always does much to
remind me of you and your jokes and i am bored/ i think/ we
all are/ and anxious to become it together and leave you
behind

i am a pig
tied up and branded
tail clipped and braided with a/ spit roast shoved clean
through me
your hands on either end and it burns/ it burns/ it burns/ i am
a dinner
a meal on a silver-plated platter served aspartame a la carte/
cigarette seasoned aside/ belonging on a table with all the
things meant to be chewed and swallowed by you/ amongst
the meats splayed out in a decorative line along the stretch
table sat twice/ ribboned strips tied bow of the angel ghosts
from before me/ their carcasses combine into a large fusion of
forgotten that stinks tooth-achingly sweet/ stinks of soured lust
for life unfulfilled i sip/ from my glass/ to look away but am
chased/ by their unfurled eyes and nerve lace i sip from my
glass and/ carrion beetles/ their bones/ look like my bones/
and i have died to realize it fully/

elolita

none of us are saved save for the trial of the tore-up
thoroughfare sign/ god bless the girls of america/ do you
know where you will go?/ god bless us all/ my eyes are
peeled grapes rolling rolling rolling across your tongue wide i
cannot look in any direction but to stare in permanent at the
destruction your unbridled affection misguiding has wrought
on both enemy and acquaintance of my heart/ it wishes
something it wishes to whisper a question in thought but
suddenly/ has never cared for anything/ not even life, i do not
care/ it was all dedicated to you in the willing memoriam of
my childhood/ never mine to give/ god bless those girls of
america/ with nobody to save us at all

a baptism at the hint of hinge in the hips
leaves a shiver there
cold in the afterbirth of lovelie'd romancings
and there i am
reflected in the darkness
reminded of the insides
reminded of their outsides
no hands may soothe the desire to
wrap my own 'round solemn
throat and leatherskin neck and crackle her all to hell in my
knuckles my palms no amount of staring at that sweet clueless
face can console me no kiss to distract my warying mind
wandering from the perhaps one little angel baby darlingest
sweet-heart is near not enough for my massive heart-hole is
still verily half loaded and leaking a gluttonous black, emptied
horrid stench these days
perhaps, perhaps…
a match of weight and not of equal qualitied grace in number
would
fix it all for a four-twine of hands must surely be abled toward
hoisting me aloft
upwards, to heaven
no more buckling or snap of spine
no more tearing in those prettied blue eyes
no more deathliness in mine, i utter i hum
for all that exists inside of perhaps

elolita

god forbid/ a tampon/ a shortened skirt/ a hair-cut, god forbid
it all/ a higher heel running a line down my left tight-stocking
that ladders paler thigh/ a novelty hobby/ an outside-ing
interest, a holy reconnection in a sip of plastic water dribbling/
out my nose before the page turned/ god forbid it all/ that i
should find you here skipping seminary to mourn my life
within the most photogenic of pews/ before it has yet even
begun to be lived/ and do forbid it all that i should learn to
walk with a straighter sway in my pigeon-footed gait/ i am
sixteen i am not the smallest size i am growth shoving through
the cracks in your finger-prison/ you should think i am
abomination unfolding/ sinking into a blackened sort/ the way
i lose my affinity for shrinking and optical illusion/ how dare i?
but i am a mirror in anger for all this change ushers itself
forward without my asking for my protruding bones to
become sheathed in a housing of fat-muscle-girl girl girl

a thin girl leads her on a sick-rotted leash takes uncertainty by
greasy chin un-made up and feeds it delusions of different
things and she routinely begs/ please, for he who loves her
like a daughter/ in his own words/ should understand she
would not will herself to face upward evolution/ she simply
cannot stop as it molds body to the tune of night and parades
screaming with a wringing grip in bone-piercing muscle-
snapping thought-threading pain pain pain/ oh, to be younger
forever/ and cuts her achilles to tighten it/ ties her stomach to
fight it/ stunts to stunt herself but she is already so old/ was
from birth/ and can smell the stinking dirt of her grave as left
foot sinks down into it/ she is lowered into it from the cloud

elolita

you were not dead this time but i still mourn myself before i
knew mourning/ before i met with strange reversing reel of
burn that somehow can hurt worse in the backwards and taste
of even more shrinking/ now when my imagination creates
you to kiss you your lips are frozen solid stinking of rotted
moisture/ death becomes you before you may even accept
that you have gone too far just too close to it/ but not yet not
yet not yet will i let it all end/ not this way/ crying out into the
hollow of a door framed with my height marked sideways
along/ not like this when/ the air you speak of as poisoned i
have not the height to taste/ stay with me/ until i can
understand why you would wish to leave

my heart/ oh, aching heart,
does it read of the beckoning
for my precious little girl to come
home again to me
only to me

elolita

skirt swishes and swirls with the boys tonight/ a dress all
sparkly blue and bubbly/ like the champagne i have never
tasted/ it is all still wrong/ the emptiness creeps its way further
up reflux'd burning throat/ i wish he could come to my
dances/ sway awkwardly with me here/ inside this stuffy
gymnasium sardine-packed with bodies the only one i yearn
to see cannot reach me past ten-thirty/ 'fore two-twelve/ sitting
the crinkle of a department store sequin puff atop the toilet
seat/ choking on mine own disarray and my friends fix their
greased hair-sprayed side parts and giggle with stupid freedom
that is glittery and dumb/ the stall smells of their perfume/
there is no escaping difference

loveless eye-follicles stationed in a permanent roaming/ there
is no warmth but the vehemence of obsession as i am
fostering some reservations heavied for the child of/ myself
and mine spirit angered/ how her temperament sways like a
detached bough load-bearing/ one vein or sinew slip away
from a clean and screeching crack/ that rips and tears and
infects the eternal scab

elolita

i cannot serve unbridled laughter that way/ for i already know
of my teeth's shaping/ already that i have vomited straight
through my chances of being beautiful for the purest sake/ for
some idiotically vacant relief/ i know he does not exist here/
but the grip of the curvature between pointer and thumb
pressed into neck-nodes has locked this jaw into a rusted
spring/ oh, and there it is - the emptiness again licking my
throat clean-lined downward/ the pains trace the veins that
pump my heart-line/ for you, it does/ and a girl can go out
and slide ill-fitting shoes along the wax-tiled floor with
company in kind/ but twisting and burning stomach-aches
remain in a way that should be questioned/ if maybe yet it is
not empty-ness at all/ but another feeling i do not yet have the
words for/ will i still feel it when you at last hold my hand/
will you ever do it?

Plumalia Henson

speaking to her
it leaves me almost captivated! such absolute stupidity
it finds me dumbfounded and joyous
how a girl can be so sparkling all throughout herself
with not a single hint of glimmering across the waters
a slant-eyed fox devil of uncertainty circling
i love it in my chest she knows it is all twisted
the knowing that she will never forget this
but how intriguingly beguiling it has become
to realize she knows not the thrill how seductive
when my gums sweat in the salivary way
a signal she must have been a delicious gift
a blessing sent earthen-bound, down in no cursing manner
never to have such purity as the day you met
but far too easily preserved under such brittled egg-shell

elolita

i am so unbelievably in love that i feel my teeth ache just from
the thought of life's sharp sweetness - nauseating in volume/ i
am in love and he loves me/ i am in love and he loves me/ i
am only knowing affection that sting with a thousand hornets
kissing/ girl in love must have nothing to say save for how
besotted, how put aside with warmth and chafing between her
legs/ the crying cicada of a plainer heart is dead/ with the
eggs not yet born of it/ and the children may have forty-eight
entire hours left to feast upon its carcass while i/ i live in
peace and spinning around 'til i am sugared sickly/ to my very
first record that skips-skips-skips/ in a skirt three sizes wrong a
cavity three sizes wrong/ a chest too large i am so desperately
in love with the stranger handsome stranger from the
telephone/ exclamation and proclamation spilling wild my
first-born language/ and he will find weariness in responding
in kind when it becomes inconveniently unsexual and too late
into the wretched nighttime for un-hungry words like 'please,
baby' but i have not yet known lacking pains/ in this
serendipitous moment/ i have not yet known love is
something to be falling out of

in my restless dreaming hours
i tuck her beneath my arm
steal her into the eternity
she kisses my cheeks in gratitude
and allows me to fuck her
as an unspoken spoken drawn-out
cam-corded thank you
in my restless waking hours
i am charged with her
i am the one she says she loves only
how beautiful
it sickens me
to be far from you
unknown homewrecker
and someday it will take me
a momentary pain to quench a
lifetime of the driest desert
stretching of grief intermingling
destroying our small oasis of
suspended lust-gaming

elolita

the older girls are so beautiful on the screen
with vein ropes hands clutching black nail polish cigarettes
dainty and lip-stained pale palm gripping obscure wine with
the bottle label turned inwards/ so messy so carefully dirtied/
refusing to allow weak imitation bars of vague censorship they
know it/ they know they are better/ they know they are so
damn cool

summer camp stole me away and dragged me/ to emptied
bleachers at nighttime sweating humidity through my tie-dyed
shirt/ my singular pair of shortest shorts/ he likes them with
the cherry-red tie up sneakers/ the ones that cut at my ankle
all high/ sang into a humid wind clothed in fourteen years of
open acoustic nothingness/ summer is always such a haze/
but i kissed her/ i remember i did/ sometimes i am so
incredibly aware of the mundane horror of a life i am living
and how stunning it could be if i might be able to thieve some
piece from the infinite casing/ to only present the moment
stretched into a life fuller how i long/ to be a film reeling with
infinite sadness made all lovely and lousy with greed age-
appropriate/ matters not/ my age is unknown/ my years are
contained within the flimsy plated frame of an overexposed
sunburn of an image/ it filters the beauty out of me and
funnels it funnel it down/ please, be pleasing

elolita

there is no worthy blood
in a bloodless world
that only exists within peach-skin
afterthought breaths
there is no worthy woman
in a woman-less world
that only exists within thirteen
unawares of love-death

in the worst years of my life
with no time left to think or eat
or breathe!
or sleep!
or dream! or find decent room cleaned out in the carcasses of
used tea-canisters, tired heart valves tumbling through empty
storage spacers begging to be utilized- fill with life, with life,
filled with memories earned
this year cannot be the worst
for the worst has already come and i
will remember his face henceforth memorized within the prints
of my body as it all fades
i will remember to pass him cleanly in the uneven street
and make no mention of my noticing his appearance
or how it resembles somebody i had known before him

elolita

the gaping yawn of my abdomen
is still sometimes shaped to fit your
loosened skin
woven like a basket puzzled to the
curvature of your weight
and my hands still web sticky to filter
your eyes
when the lights are just too bright/
though i cannot even recall the color of
them/
and my entire body is still made to/
dissolve milky-white antacid into
your morning tea, how perfectly warmed
and when i look at myself
scrubbed raw and freshly bathed
all i see is you, smoother, kinder/
most consistent,
most talented,
most sparkling and/
most/ most-
most of it all/
of all more than me/
what if i cannot find my way back?
what if the curlicue of the path twists up
in my aching head
and the fear devours me
alone in this wood-
with the string gone slack from
some creature gnawing at it
one i had known by name and bed
but now want not to associate with

would you look for me?
would you recognize the curvature of
my strange
flattened step-weight amongst the
animal prints- though they are much
heavier now
/by breast and by heart/
or mark me on a wooden cross beside
the southernmost
highway and bear me a wreath of
plastic floral
lamenting nothing but the money
spent to mourn me
would you see me in how i had
changed/ and regret being one to
change me?

elolita

i need no mirror with which to see
the way my hair curls beneath my jaw
i was born with little eyes all around
swirling and twirling and forever projecting
within me what is outside
my figure is my viewing platform
my breast a pulpit from which i stare into a
cathedrallic hall of mirrors
a priestess of hateful devotion and remorseful
masturbation in my stroking of the soul for any shining of
hopeful survival among the weeds of wretched age
and i wonder at times
when the air is cold in that way that prickles skin
and draws ash if the men
who told tales of my mind-bent and unscrewed disposition
were in fact not liars and slanderers
coaxing hot hatred from my peers
but a band of prophets
and even when i am feeling nothing
the nothing is so much of something that i
feel maybe it was never actually nothing
but some emotion that i have not named

you'll find me being
softened by time
in the prickly atmosphere of it all
for a flower that swallows
cleaned and tight-fisted
finds infinite flexibility so
as to never succumb to a choke
and what of my rage-
but what within it
could create an ascension that
defies all my lotion-skinned
limitations-
and what of my body-
but what a heart inside
could pour love from any harsh-stabbed
passerby's drinking spigot placed
with zero ovation, a servant
but no punishment either, so
a lonely little princess instead

elolita

i am struggling to find fairness within this life
how it weighs and bows me down to my knees
with whiplash-ed force
and you say there is none, life is not fair
but what is living without a balance
when the dirt soaks the rain up as thirstily
as the clouds ache to give it
and the money that i spend is a definite
value when measured in proportion
to the joyous pleasure i receive when
devouring my meals like the animal at the tree-line
there is fairness in that mother
but my chemistry leaves me wanting
for something i know i would despise when
acquiring it
i am forever fifteen/ finding feral sustenances within older
boys/ men/ but really, boys/ and bending my body to the
lyrics of some song that details the futures i don't dare caress/
with any tongue of imagination/ and i am eternally seven/
hoping to someday scrub myself hard enough with the shower
brush-bristles
and burn my skin into oblivion so that/ i may emerge some
glistening pearl-egg of a woman and catch my shiny straight/
hair along the breeze as it embraces me and never trips me
over
there is fairness there, maybe
in that the thick tears of a dreamer may
water the gardens of those who never learned
to be wanton and desperate
i find a potential truth emerging from my tired rind-
that maybe the balance is within me already

77

in ensuring that
by wanting forever to be embraced by all things
i may never receive it, and in wanting to
be warmed to my bones by a tired bathing
i must always be the one to draw it

elolita

take a photo of me smoking a cigarette fated for the stomp of
my boot as the flash dies/ take a photo of me hanging my
legs into a black abyss while you grip my spine away from
eyes/ afraid/ photograph me photographing myself in the
clothes i hide beneath my bed so i can take them off/
photograph that, too/ immortalize me/ immortalize me/
immortalize me/ immortalize me

there is a bruise-d apple slipped sweetly between your lip and gum/ nameless and shapeless being that slut is created in the kiln of wanton yearning and cooled in the wet of insanity insatiable/ it is possible that slut may be nothing at all/ certainly nothing important/ but you cannot hide/ it is important to you/ so you must declare it/ say it/ say it again/ again/ again/ agai-/ claim the mess you have made as your own collared creation a mistake a half-clothed beggar at your door with wearied hungried hands cupped for you/ a small pet of an animal lying in wait sheathed in slutty sequin and slutty eyeshadow stick dollar-store half-smudged melting/ digging itself out of the inviting bed to beg for you to just want it/ beg for it/ already/ before it saws off its secondary sex and sticks it into the oven burn away the fat and love and wanting of someone who has everything to provide but kindness/ flaccid boredom it is/ and that slut wants love/ stupid little girl-slut love/ you had said it so clearly deserved a starring role

elolita

three-
two-
one-
and i am rendered unraveling
all that can be flows flows flows into me/ so much open-
mouthed bliss my entire body a net to capture hope as it
springs from the beading of her brow
my entire mind a jailer-savior-king

maybe there could have been joy there/ and maybe i could have found it in those shaking shadow moments of feigned independence and inside-outside peace/ i felt truth/ never having failed until i lay crushed beneath the weighing of my life and yours all stitch-ed up together/ and i did engage in hush-ed tones around the dining table/ i told them all about this time/ how it was different/ but they did not know either/ whatever could lie beyond this reeling wheeling cycle of love hate love again, love again/ of fondness and cruelty and the hilt that wields retreating

elolita

weep, oh smaller darling
for the veins of it all are bruising
this body you built
and the frailty you so often pose
in a confident stature and demure turn
some boastful echo to ease your
fear of being a looser style of woman
is killing you mercilessly
the beauty of running fingernail beneath
rotted fingernail and scraping away the
blackened dirt is that it all is done by only you,
both dirty and wretched-wrung but
pure? pure? pure?
weep, what blood runs through this river
and what of it did i drink
to run this red all down my neck
and face a breasted peak
the biting iron does call and call
with silent scream of a begging screech
the wound,
the wound,
the wound
it cries
but my gasping
prevents that i speak

in buttery beating of my
sleep-addled
heart i found
the slickened bulbs of
nature's fresh weakness
sitting quickly still uncaged
and there was
something horribly terribly
romantic within him
within his palm,
some arc-ed stage
a phrase that of which i
could never forget
a love that could never
be surgically removed
i found a bend within
my straightest bone
and the crackle sounded
throughout my ears
and he could hear
it echoed still, through
cartilage and sweeping tear

elolita

sometimes to smile is a slicing of the lip/ a cutting of the
cheek to cheek that makes your worst part speak/ but the
baring of the teeth is but a wicked, cursed display to reveal
the gruesome nature of your heart/ and the web of plaque-d
sinew flesh that rests/ in a weave of browning hard-stuff
between your tooth and gum/ to be a girl and smile is smart/
to be a woman and smile is dumb and
oh, it is all the same, the same/ to find it so contraire/ for what
smile could truly turn a tide/ of some stranger possess-ed
devilman, there/ what flick of hair and swish of breast could/
truly turn the curse of death and for why, for who, for where/
to be natural and bend as the tree in beckoning to a bullet-
train force wind/ to be natural and flutter a butterfly lash is a
criminal offense in the eyes of his sex

Plumalia Henson

what am i meant to do now, lover/ with this mind you hold in
such regard/ think about it?
i fear if that becomes reality i may never/ see you again/ not
with these blackened hands that reach
into depths of soot and ash to claw out some/ sweeter portrait
of us/ not as you once were, no/
i would become forever changed to/ find words within my
head to mold you/ you rotted experience/ the little love-dove
knows not what to sing of, what to fly towards/ when the
gently brutalistic finger of grief has tore its nest and turned it
tooth-picking/ why can you not just find me in the little
between-space where my head would rest/ that soft
hammocking of skin connecting shoulder and arm and torso
that i nestle against with such feverish desire to be loved/ why
can you not understand me when all you have done has been
to study my body? did you not find the secret of my weakness
lingering in the pixel-ated shadow behind my bare chest, my
ribbed torso un-fed? could you not see my love spelled out for
you within the little web-cracklings in the pattern of my bitten
fingernails as they reached/ reached/ reached for you? and
now i must cry my prayers of daddy and heart-wrencher into
the oblivious nighttime air, for the original one has done his
responding and un-pinned me from the floral wall-paper to
flutter endlessly towards the ground

elolita

he left me/ he left me and the world is so cold against my
heart all broken/ all opened to accept it/ it burns all the way
through/ he left me/ he left me and i find no solace in
strangers shaped like him, find no interest in training myself to
the desperate flexing inflexible whim of another leering gaze/
he left me/ and now my life is become divided into a before
and an after/ and the other man does speak of touching me,
but it is not the same/
i do not feel compelled, magical/
 special, inherently/
has fifteen always felt
this greasy/ this ugly/
this awkward, unloved?
he left me/ a little girl/ alone
and all i know are strangers now

Plumalia Henson

teeth gnash and clash/ to fight to find to whip the bone to
mash/ and it all falls so elegantly down a slickened softened
palate, there where a rhinestone-decorated esophagus tubes a
loop a loop a loop of squelching flesh/ every bolus an
offering to the/ body born from transgression and the fight of
living is nothing pure/ not elegant or fine-the fires of life have
left me tore clean in halves of halves of halves down my
center-folded line-to find it all a little amusing is simply not
allowed by rule/ but divinity strikes no easy lover/ no gentler
than you/ to pound and pound and pound and slap and break
and hurt and cradle me-and another blood curse wretch has
made her solemn tendrils stretch/ and stretch and stretch and
stretch across the world in wave formation/ a consistent
pulposus flow/ so all light that bears the heart of man must
carry a red-stain within its/ tiresome television glow/
unrelenting like the watchful gaze of a man, which you are/
not

elolita

the way the white-oiled swan greases its own throat with
sliver'd teeth and feminine glare glancing off of her purest
body of light/ the way the waters glitter and ripple and fold
like melting dough of glass over and over top of each other
relentlessly/ the way i run barefoot along the pavement until
my feet are flattened black/ trying to sweat you out/ trying to
keep the warmth of you in. i cannot speak to you in these
moments- i find no attraction to the idea of slicing my throat
open and letting the reflux drip and drizzle from my open cuts
for you, so you may lick them from bare chest and tell me
what regret tastes like/ i already know/ i taste it every day
because of you/ because of you/ because of you

if you close your eyes the cigarettes almost smell like a
wildfire/ the wine almost smells like its ancestor-mother/ you
are next to me, and i spray your perfume against my side so i
may feel you in the dampness/ i sprayed too much/ it never
lasts. cheap alcohol fragrances consume me/ go ahead and do
the same. suckle on the sweet tang of a murder weapon and
pretend it tastes metallic in the way of a life-blood and not the
way of a punctuative form undignified and infected/ while i
recognize the brutality of the truth that if i do not/ remember
this/ write it down, convey/ conform/ control it all/ my soul
may expire due within a hot snap on a doily bed and a tied
screech/ and i may expire due within the hour i may bang my
fists on my knees to see a bruise to wind a color palette that
in theory is beautiful and in my eyes is perfection
encapsulated within the seventy-eight pounds of me, bleeding/
until i am bled/ a past figment/ a passing fractal

elolita

what man is strong enough to tell a little heart
with its tiny beatings and bleatings that it must
bear the fruitage of a life poorly lived and simply led-
led by chain-links by his father's missed calls into a
wet hole of damp beneath the ground
where she wishes to picnic
but i have courage-
and confidence, too!
this is sufficient for my propping
my maintaining
she knows just how to liquify herself
into that intravenous solution
glowing milky pure
and swim down-tube to me
to me, to me, again again again-
electrify me! how it does
the caffeinated bubble
and i pinch it with finger and fore-
swallowing delight and exhaling discarded
miseries straight into her eyes-
she can take it!
she can take it, as i will it
as i defend it with all twenty digits bared
clutching my slick perch atop her chest
to protect her heart, of course;
of course!

fifteen candles blazing
one of them/ the fifteenth/ it burns my hair
And i wish to say i did not make it occur, but my fingers still
hover pale and webbed/ still pinching the strand/ watching
the chemical blonde-d wisp blacken and burn before me and
stink a stench of something foul
this year, my delusion so pure is my closest companion/ this
year, i am my sole lover for it is not him as him but him as a
player within mine own writings/ a love interest within the
velvety-oranged curtains of my mind that play out such
weighted scenes to myself- such a devoted audience/ and how
comical it must have been, to see a thin-but-not-skinny little
girl turned sickly teenager in that trademarked sense/ as she
lay still as death becoming on her bed/ staring at the ceiling
with that youthful escapism in all intention to see anything
but/ anything but how the paint peels/ the orange light
reddening brown does nothing to complement the blue tones
of my skin and it is a shame, then/ how my birthday goes un-
witnessed/ even the instant camera is not allowed to blink
within the fogged view-finder/ a scene worth staging is no
scene here/ no scene at all, to live un-watched and un-
regarded

elolita

i dreamt of him mid-day/ an occurrence not unusual but
distressing like a roaring rapid river sweeping me back the
way i had been violently thrashing and splashing/ fighting
with all my weight to escape/ his presence does not leave me
my romantic man-ghost/ even in lethargy, my mind races and
buzzes like a little angered wasp through pictures, images of
him/ his wrist/ his hands/ his veins/ the side of his face, so
blessed to contain/ the corner of such an eye, so willful and
watching/ i dreamt of a protector dripping kerosene from my
lamp to set my entire home alight/ and i wrote it into a poem/
and spit it into the unforgiving slant ether of a glittering
universe where every girl but myself owns their own star in
the night sky, and every man has bitten a chunk out of the
singular moon to leak it into their throats/ and called it love,
they called it that

what finality eludes me
to never meet the one who has borne much of my heart/
molded my pink clay within ash-dusted hands, printed my
skin/ age before age after age/ with notes of critique and
criticism my mother could never touch, though she/ may/ she
may try- what of my conclusion? what of the warmth before
my slumber, and where shall i lay when it all is done/ when
will it be done? For he seemed to be finished but i am still/
budding/ budding/ budding and it-
is not my fault/ that he seems to have the future-vision of a
cynic obsessed with the sexuality of death, how he sees me/
pre-de-composed/ dead before deceased/ and never flush
with life, as it does drip from my paling lips in salivary
strands/ he never fears touching me and braving the slough
of sun-dried flesh against living/ but he no longer whines to
kiss my soured lips/ claims it is gross to touch a dead girl/
claims me unholy, possessed in potentiality and physicality
quite like a witch

elolita

in bellows and breaks
of tainted breath withering
the quivering of her lips
the shake over bended knee
it is all so incredibly suggestive
a trained seductress

the whiskey-sweet hot breath warms my cheeks and flushes
my features/ i am fractured/ i am frozen/ fitted out in a
fashion that is not my own but slides over my skin in a
mimicking silk when i dress thirteen i am dressed nine and
when i dress fourteen i am dressed twenty-two and the inches
between my knee and my hip seem to be stretched over his
eyes like some blindfold protecting him from the fact that i am
some taboo artifact/ i am some little leaf, to be flitting between
the bricks that squeeze tight the foundation of any house i
cannot bear to be trapped in/ i cannot bear to be trapped/ but
his cages are plush and warm like the womb of a crossed
arm/ so it cannot possibly be the same/ i sense with all my
mature instinct when guided beneath his heavy hand that/ this
is very different/ i chose to tumble my bare body down this
little hole/ i chose to bruise at the bottom/ and i choose to
keep cleanliness alive beneath my fingernails by never/ never/
never choosing to claw myself out

elolita

he will never love again.
please, lord in heaven and in my backyard-
steal his sacred heart/ bury it with me/ when he kills me? and
i swear i heard my god sigh/ and i swear i felt the earth nod/
yes, i will/ for even my messiah has abandoned my dealing of
fate as it lays splayed out in unreadable cards on the sickening
velvet rope of cold thigh/ even the magdalene cannot foresee
a way in which i light myself a guide from this tepid darkness/
she only knows to tuck me in, and leave the door cracked/ so
i may taste/taste/taste the freedom, smell it/ but never yet feel
that innocent warmth on my saturated skin/ so may he never
love again

Plumalia Henson

do you believe in god/ God?/ in that firstly creating of us all/
he was made only just before/ so little girls may find their
paths set linear and scenic within the curves that grace his
face/ and comfort themselves in the folded bend of his elbow/
the star sprinkled down as bright white powdered sugar to
shape him on wet-fresh dough so he may care for me/ catch
me i did slip into an awkward tumbling-down from the
birthing way/ so i would not catch loneliness here for, oh/
how terror holds and oh,/ how warming in the abdomen to
free yourself from thought and instead rest your twin braided
headed on the shoulder of a buzzard so wild/ and feel only a
gentile nature in how his razor beak snaps at bones for all but
you/ god is in there/ god made that

elolita

my sensuality is a gun/ meant to be directed at him, at him/
but i seem to be far too often finding myself staring/ straight
down the barrel/ the long black wave of gray and powder/
my sensuality is a grenade/ for which i have long lost the pin/
before being shuttered inside this solitary box/ i shone so
brightly you could have been blinded/ but now i am/ killing
myself/ without lifting a finger in malice/ just stretching my
weary frame/ to love him as much/ as much/ as i possibly
can/ and it is honestly, not that much/ and the effort leaves
me stranded in a dry desert of exhaustion/ i am too tired to
hike up my skirt in your direction any longer/ but i do it
anyways, and that-that is the gun/ spraying blood and pain
and muscle and bruising the air as it fires between my teeth

Plumalia Henson

dignity sits before us, now
as a lamb's head perched atop an unraveling cushion of sinew
and cord/ weeping marrow/ weeping blood/ weeping
weeping weeping/ but when i cry to him, beg for forgiveness
he unbraids the piglet-plaits my mother had sewn to my scalp
with her loveless fingers/ and says there is nothing to forgive/
for he likes me better in that light, he says, and he appreciates
my trying, he says, and he/ he/ he finds me/ absolutely
beguiling, he says/ but this feeling of ushering in a new age
has become fearfully transparent and terribly naked i do not
know how to pose for such twisted words/ when all my body
feels painfully unfurled against a biting wind/ and all my skin
is burning

elolita

i am learning the art of not knowing/ i feel my humanity
grows lesser with every anxious question answered/ stale
thought bleeding my eternal pen dry everything causes cancer
everything wrinkles me everything makes me cry/ drags me
even further from you/ sometimes i feel lucky/ you cannot see
me except for my pristine rehearsal except for the tops of my
thighs in a pale blue sheen except for the sheen of my hair
ringing behind my collar-bones shoved frontward like a star/
deep wells of skin that you once asked if i could hold pennies
in/ and i could/ and i cried/ i am just a jester of starvation and
stupidity at times parading/ my sickness for you while my hair
is stroked and we play pretend-comforting and you do
actually comfort me/ maybe/ but only when i can play dumbly
ignorant to dance and swing my arms as if a partner curl my
fingers as if held tight in yours/ smile alone to the blank facing
wall where i imagine you leaning/ a genuine blush to my
features so enlivening/ so embalming/ so embarrassing to be
in love with the white wicker emptiness

the gingerbread house sits stale/ i wonder of its expiration/
has it passed?/ should i throw the glitter-tossed walls and
gumdrop lovers in the trash? he won't speak/ what have i
done in all my malignant defiance/ to have my hands feel so
wet, always with his blood/ always with his tears/ always with
his saccharine sweat as his palms grip mine so tightly/ strain
my shoulders 'til they are free-folding blades winged and torn
straight from my freckled back-skin/ and good for having him/
had i otherwise not known/ how heartbreaking little girls
apparently can grow to be when they get everything they
want/ and how cruel i apparently have been/ to not return the
favor of a sacrificial sweetness

elolita

three-
two-
one-
and i turn it on
that which flows flows flows from me
all the wide-eyeing twitch charm
my entire body an open palm
my entire mind a void

what a peculiar turning of the rusted wheel
not yet perceived as fragile to feel so/ energetic every
encounter twinkling glowing owl bright amidst the endless/
yet in the suddens/ no longer a collector no more/ merely i
am a surveyor a life-bleeding catalogue/ friendship has lost all
romance by way of asphyxiation and time and time and time/
does crawl on until i am no creature but hands and knees
printed on pavement and grass towards home/ where he calls
for me/ silently

elolita

the woman of the womb can never escape her distending
cousin/ she is forever entangled with/ entrapped by/ the Vein/
she has never been jealous of her elders i have never found
peace in shining my head-lamp into their milk fleshe-ed
sclera/ discovery of mine own fate is no easy button to mend/
never-mind with frilled embellishments rounding the edge of
inescapable/ she has never been jealous of her elders/ but
now i am concerned i may be learning it/ of the nesting
dollies i had buried/ oh, i wish i could dig into the mud and
rub my eyes with visions/ she spent all loose pocket years on
watching the fragile flutter burlesque of vodka retching and
rolling eyes acid-washed denim/ her memories are none her
own

there is only fear harvesting the body here/ first-phobic form
sweating with every milestone passed so quickly so
excruciating/ will i be afraid of you, when all is said and done
and writ in the concrete/ devastatingly sloppy finger curls/
when you decide you must abandon me/ my first/ love?/ oh, i
cannot even hardly bear to speak of the when, oh/ how i wish
i could outstretch the bones of my fragmented ribs wing-ed
beneath my breasts to carry optimism past an ounce/ oh, i
could extend our love affair deeper into the forgetful blues
and blacks of such fleeting night/ i love you even when/ i fear
it/ it kills me/ i still do/ only frightens me more

elolita

what a big man/ what big hands/ and massive plans to sweep
me away/ but no dream pushes the wheel/ just an urge to
shove under the pretty woven rug/ and all the blood

Plumalia Henson

an alarm rings
nobody hears it i am/ too accustomed
to the wrong you make me feel/ my
legs have forgotten how to
run from my heart's cruel magnet

elolita

the sir treats me handsome/ he acts toward me kind and
gentle/ giving with the fork that carries all sweetness it could
be feigned/ the brightest red strawberries from the super
market floor perched delicately atop tongue/ a patient
cardinal/ and yet i do not believe he knows i would slaughter
at his request/ all the while begging for him to leash me by
my hair and swallow me entirely so i may go wherever he
goes/ know whomever he knows/ and die his every death
alongside him, purely one

Plumalia Henson

if the earth were a communion wafer
i would chase him right down the edge
wine-stained lips love-stained eyes
i would follow him right down with
un-crossed arms spread out wide
all of it would be ours
all of him would be mine

elolita

he is so beautiful just like the man on the magazines at the
pediatrician's office/ all scruffy and gentle as a brown bear in a
children's book/ he says i am too young for him/ but he purrs
it like it delights/ and he still twinkles ever bright in the bleeds
of late to early/ could peace possibly exist in his shape?/ i dare
to find out if i may peel back the sweatied nylon polyester
denim skins the uniform of a working man in the same
tumbling washing machine as my/ under-garments/ my school
clothes/ something like our hands laid on top of each other/
in inane measurement of wisdom/ inches of safety i find from
it/ inches away from salvation i find within it

such stupid girls
necks all swan-crooked at the tall table/ fingers and brows
knitted led to the doggie-bowl by authors politickers post-haze
grown ups synonymous with foolishness/ hand-fed the
loosening tug that drops organs unbuckled leashing ribbon-
type rope-type thing fingered/ by a lazing hand on a shine
screen/ standard in issue transportable in size/ the thinnest of
onion skin to carry/ mothering lips open in slottish shape/ a
tube for her withering tones in their minds they consider
themselves so misunderstood/ as if sixteens is an unresearched
affliction/ the dead pile up woven into a basket of wicker
beneath the grave shadow of a twisted orange/ longing still for
the color of the days when peeling yourself made you a starlet
and not poorly managed/ but there is a certain thing to be
declared for floating above the southern fogs across the lake
that looms so wide and gnawing/ they rot together at last

www.ingramcontent.com/pod-product-compliance
Lightning Source LLC
Chambersburg PA
CBHW021338140626
46545CB00020B/2368